NATURAL PÂTÉS

A tasty collection of wholefood pâtés and spreads,
suitable for every occasion from picnic to dinner party.

In the same series
NATURAL BISCUITS
NATURAL SPICES
NATURAL SWEETS

By the same author
ITALIAN VEGETARIAN COOKING

NATURAL PÂTÉS

by

Jo Marcangelo

Illustrated by Clive Birch

THORSONS PUBLISHERS LIMITED
Wellingborough, Northamptonshire

First published 1984

© JO MARCANGELO 1984

British Library Cataloguing in Publication Data

Marcangelo, Jo
   Natural pâtés.
   1. Vegetable pates (Cookery)
   I. Title
   641.6'5   TX801

   ISBN 0-7225-0937-5

Reproduced, printed and bound in Great Britain by
Hazell Watson & Viney Limited,
Member of the BPCC Group,
Aylesbury, Bucks

CONTENTS

INTRODUCTION

Pâté is good eaten almost any time of the day; so there is nothing more comforting than having 'something on hand' in your refrigerator for the first course, light lunch or to have with drinks for unexpected visitors. Most vegetable pâtés and spreads will keep in the refrigerator for up to three weeks, especially if they are sealed with a little melted butter or margarine. Many of them freeze well too, so you can keep one in the freezer for emergencies!

Vegetable pâtés or purées, as they are sometimes called in restaurants, are extremely simple to make and with today's blenders and food processors can be made in next to no time. However, not all the recipes included need a blender or food processor — just a sharp knife and perhaps a sieve or a hand operated food mill to purée vegetables.

Pâtés, spreads and terrines are the perfect food for picnics, summer buffet parties or a starter for a dinner party at any time of the year. Terrines make attractive centrepieces on a buffet table or served in slices. You do, however, need a little patience and time to assemble the various layers of vegetables and filling, but it is a satisfying and not too difficult task if you set yourself a morning free. Their main advantage, if you are entertaining, is that all the time-consuming preparation is out of the way well in advance — even a day or two before — so that on the day you can devote all your time to other dishes without having to worry about the first course.

Natural wholefood ingredients are included in all the recipes. Most vegetables, beans and nuts can be used to produce vegetarian pâtés and spreads and with the addition of breadcrumbs, grains, cereals, and herbs and spices the possibilities are endless. Vegetable pâtés and spreads are light and when eaten with wholemeal bread are very nourishing, especially those which include beans, lentils, cheese or yogurt.

There is sometimes confusion between the definition of a pâté and a terrine. What in English is called a pâté, the French call *terrine*. Technically speaking, a pâté is enclosed in a pastry case (from pâté — pastry), whilst a terrine is named after the container in which it is cooked, originally an earthenware (terra — earth) dish with a lid. In France, too, the difference between pâté and terrine is slowly disappearing and the words are interchangeable. Through common usage though, the word terrine now tends to be used for a pâté with layers in it, such as the vegetable terrines found on page 32 and 36. These are built up from layers of different ingredients embedded in a mousse or savoury custard mixture to reveal strips of contrasting colours and textures when sliced.

Terrines based on vegetables are fresh, light and colourful. You can make a terrine from only two or three vegetables, or a great variety, according to taste and time of year. When choosing vegetables bear in mind appearance as well as texture and flavour. In addition, choose vegetables of varied shapes and colours that will look attractive in cross-section when the terrine is sliced.

A terrine dish is usually a long, deep dish with a lid made of earthenware, steel or enamelled cast-iron and more recently of ovenproof glass. However, a 2 lb (900g) loaf tin or any deep-sided dish like a soufflé dish can be used instead, with foil or buttered greaseproof paper improvising for the lid. To ensure gentle, even cooking to set the ingredients, a terrine is best cooked in a *bain marie*, i.e. in a roasting pan filled with hot water to come halfway up the dish. Terrines that are based on vegetables do not improve with keeping; in order to make the most of their fresh ingredients, they are best served the day after they are made.

A good way to start a dinner party is with a plate of crudités and one or two dishes of vegetarian dips or pâtés. These allow your guests to pick and nibble leisurely whilst continuing the conversation, which is, after all, what a good dinner party is all about.

PÂTÉS AND TERRINES

BLACK-EYED BEAN PÂTÉ

½ lb (225g) black-eyed beans, soaked overnight
4 tablespoonsful olive oil
1 medium onion, finely chopped
1 stick of celery, finely chopped
1-2 cloves of garlic, peeled and crushed
1½-2 tablespoonsful tomato purée
½ teaspoonful dried basil
½ teaspoonful dried oregano
Sea salt and freshly ground black pepper

1. Drain the beans, place them in a pan and cover with cold water. Bring to the boil and simmer for 1 hour, or until tender.

2. Heat the oil in a pan, add the onion, celery and garlic and fry for 8-10 minutes until softened. Stir in the tomato purée and herbs and cook for a few minutes.

3. Drain the beans and mash them well. Combine all the ingredients and season to taste. Turn into a serving dish and leave to cool. Serve with fingers of wholemeal toast and a side salad.

Serves 4.

2 lbs (900g) courgettes
Sea salt
2 oz (50g) butter or polyunsaturated margarine
3 eggs
⅓ pint (200ml) single cream
Freshly grated nutmeg
Freshly ground black pepper

To garnish:

½ red pepper
Sprigs of parsley

1. Wash and trim the courgettes, then grate coarsely using a hand grater or food processor. Place in a large mixing bowl, add 1 tablespoonful of salt and toss well. Leave to stand for about 1 hour for the salt to draw out their liquid.

2. Squeeze the courgettes with your hands to remove as much liquid as possible. Melt the butter or margarine in a large frying pan, add the courgettes and cook for 7 to 8 minutes until soft. Leave to cool.

3. Whisk the eggs and cream together, add the courgettes and season with salt, pepper and nutmeg to taste.

4. Line a 2 lb (900g) capacity loaf tin with non-stick vegetable parchment or greaseproof paper. Pour the

mixture into the prepared tin and cover with buttered greaseproof paper. Place in a baking dish filled with hot water to come halfway up the tin. Bake in a preheated moderate oven, 350°F/180°C (Gas Mark 4) for 1¼ hours or until set and firm. Allow the terrine to settle for 10 minutes before removing from the tin. Cool and refrigerate overnight. Garnish with strips of red pepper, sprigs of parsley and serve with wholemeal toast.

Serves 6.

CLIVE BIRCH

NUT AND LENTIL PÂTÉ

¾ lb (350g) mixed nuts, ground
4 oz (100g) cooked brown lentils (dry weight)
4 oz (100g) fresh wholemeal breadcrumbs
2 oz (50g) butter or polyunsaturated margarine
1 large onion, finely chopped
4 sticks of celery, finely chopped
1-2 cloves of garlic, peeled and crushed
2 teaspoonsful tomato purée
3 eggs
⅓ pint (200ml) home-made tomato sauce
1 level teaspoonful dried thyme
½ level teaspoonful dried oregano
Sea salt and freshly ground black pepper

1. Mix together the nuts, lentils and breadcrumbs in a bowl.

2. Melt the butter or margarine in a pan. Add the onion, celery and garlic and fry for 4 minutes until softened. Stir in the tomato purée and cook for a further 2-3 minutes. Take out of the pan and add to the nut, lentil and crumb mixture.

3. Beat the eggs with the tomato sauce, herbs and salt and pepper. Pour into the ingredients in the bowl, mixing very thoroughly.

4. Press the mixture into a greased 2 lb (900g) loaf tin. Cook in a preheated oven, 375°F/190°C (Gas Mark 5) for 1½-2 hours or until set.

5.   Allow to cool completely before removing the pâté from the tin. Serve chilled with slices of wholemeal toast or bread.

Serves 6-8.

CREAM CHEESE AND CASHEW NUT PÂTÉ

4 oz (100g) broken cashew nut pieces
½ lb (225g) cream cheese
4 tablespoonsful yogurt
1 clove of garlic, peeled and crushed (optional)
1 tablespoonful fresh parsley, finely chopped
Sprigs of fresh parsley to garnish

1.   Roast the cashew nut pieces lightly under the grill or in the oven.

2.   Grind the nuts in an electric coffee grinder, nut mill or food processor, until quite fine.

3.   Beat together the cheese and yogurt, stir in the ground nuts, together with the garlic (if using) and parsley and mix well.

4.   Press into individual ramekin dishes, cover and refrigerate until required. Garnish with sprigs of fresh parsley.

Note: This can also be used as a spread or sandwich filler.

Serves 4-6.

LENTIL PÂTÉ

½ lb (225g) brown lentils
1 bay leaf
3 oz (75g) butter
1 large onion, finely chopped
1 clove of garlic, peeled and crushed
6 oz (175g) mushrooms, finely chopped
1-2 tablespoonsful tahini (sesame paste)
½ teaspoonful dried thyme
½ teaspoonful dried marjoram
Juice of 1 lemon
Sea salt and freshly ground black pepper

1. Wash the lentils and pick them over for stones. Place in a pan with the bay leaf and cover with cold water. Bring to the boil, cover and simmer for 50 minutes to 1 hour or until the lentils are tender. Drain well, then purée in a blender or push through a sieve.

2. Melt ⅔ of the butter in a pan, add the onion and garlic and fry until softened. Add the mushrooms and cook for a further 2-3 minutes.

3. Mix all the ingredients together and adjust the seasoning to taste. Turn into a serving dish or individual dishes and smooth surface. Leave to cool.

4. Melt the remaining butter in a small pan, pour over top of pâté. Chill well before serving with fingers of wholemeal toast.

Serves 4-6.

STILTON AND WALNUT PÂTÉ

1 oz (25g) butter
1 oz (25g) wholemeal flour
7 fl oz/⅓ pint (200ml) milk
4 oz (100g) Stilton cheese, crumbled
1 tablespoonful mayonnaise
2 oz (50g) chopped walnuts
1 clove of garlic, peeled and crushed (optional)
Sea salt and freshly ground black pepper

1. Melt the butter in a saucepan, stir in the flour and cook for 1 minute. Gradually add the milk and bring to the boil. Cook for 2-3 minutes, stirring constantly until thickened. Remove from the heat and stir in the cheese. Leave to cool.

2. Add the mayonnaise, walnuts, garlic (if using) and seasoning to taste. Mix well.

3. Spoon into four individual ramekin dishes, cover and refrigerate until required. Garnish with walnut halves and serve with fingers of wholemeal toast.

Serves 4.

MUSHROOM PÂTÉ

2 oz (50g) butter or polyunsaturated margarine
1 medium onion, finely chopped
1 lb (450g) button mushrooms
½ lb (225g) fresh wholemeal breadcrumbs
4 oz (100g) mixed nuts, ground
1 egg, well beaten
1 teaspoonful yeast extract
1 teaspoonful mixed herbs of choice
Seasoning to taste

To garnish:

1 bunch of watercress, washed and trimmed
Wedges of tomato

1. Melt the butter or margarine in a frying pan. Add the onion and fry until soft but not browned — about 5 minutes.

2. Add the mushrooms and cook over a gentle heat until most of the liquid evaporates. Stir the mixture frequently to make sure it does not stick to the pan.

3. Cool slightly, then reduce the onion and mushroom mixture to a smooth purée in a blender or food processor. Transfer to a mixing bowl.

4. Add all the remaining ingredients and mix well. Taste and adjust the seasoning, then spoon the pâté into a 1 lb (450g) buttered loaf tin. Cover with foil and bake

in a preheated moderate oven, 350°F/180°C (Gas Mark 4) for about 1 hour.

5. Chill well and turn out on to a serving dish. Garnish with watercress and wedges of tomato and serve with wholemeal toast or bread.

Serves 6-8.

SWISS CHEESE AND VEGETABLE PÂTÉ

3 oz (75g) butter or polyunsaturated margarine
1 large onion, finely chopped
1-2 cloves of garlic, peeled and crushed
12 oz (350g) button mushrooms, finely chopped
1 lb (450g) carrots, finely grated
8 oz (225g) Gruyère or Emmental cheese, finely grated
4 oz (100g) cashew nuts, finely ground
4 eggs, well beaten
1 level teaspoonful dried thyme
½ level teaspoonful dried oregano
Sea salt and freshly ground black pepper

1. Melt the butter or margarine in a large frying pan. Add the onion and garlic and fry until soft but not browned — about 5 minutes.

2. Add the mushrooms, cover and cook for 5 minutes. Uncover and cook, stirring, until most of the liquid has evaporated. Cool slightly, then liquidize the contents of the pan in a blender or food processor. Transfer to a mixing bowl.

3. Add all the remaining ingredients and mix well. Season with salt and pepper to taste.

4. Press the mixture into a buttered 2 lb (900g) loaf tin. Place in a roasting pan half-filled with boiling water. Cook in a preheated moderate oven, 350°F/180°C

(Gas Mark 4) for 1¼-1½ hours or until set. Chill until
ready to serve.

Serves 6-8.

AUBERGINE PÂTÉ

1 large aubergine (about ½ lb/225g)
½ lb (225g) cream cheese
4-5 spring onions (white part only, finely chopped)
1 tomato, skinned, deseeded and chopped
1 tablespoonful fresh parsley, chopped
2 tablespoonsful olive oil
Sea salt and freshly ground black pepper

To garnish:

Chopped parsley
Black olives

1. Bake aubergine as described on page 62. Cool, peel,
   then mash the flesh and mix into the softened cream
   cheese. Stir in the spring onions, tomato, parsley, oil
   and salt and pepper to taste; mix well.

2. Turn into a serving dish and chill. Serve garnished
   with chopped parsley and black olives, if liked.

Serves 4.

CURRIED SPLIT PEA PÂTÉ

2 tablespoonsful vegetable oil
1 medium onion, finely chopped
2 medium carrots, finely chopped
1 tablespoonful curry powder
½ lb (225g) green split peas, soaked overnight and
   drained
1 bay leaf
1 pint (570ml) stock or water
Seasoning
2 tablespoonsful fresh coriander or parsley, chopped

1. Heat the oil in a saucepan, add the onion and carrots
   and fry until the onion is transparent. Stir in the curry
   powder and cook for a few minutes.

2. Add the split peas, bay leaf and stock or water. Bring
   to the boil, reduce heat and simmer for about 45
   minutes. There should be little or no liquid left.

3. Remove the bay leaf. Blend to a purée in a blender
   or push through a sieve. Taste and adjust the
   seasoning.

4. Turn into a serving dish and leave in a cool place for
   30 minutes. Sprinkle with chopped coriander or
   parsley just before serving.

Serves 4.

VEGETABLE PÂTÉ

4 oz (100g) brown lentils
1 medium carrot, finely chopped
1 medium parsnip, finely chopped
1 bay leaf
2 tablespoonsful vegetable oil
1 medium onion, finely chopped
4 oz (100g) mushrooms, chopped
2 teaspoonsful mixed herbs
2 teaspoonsful tomato purée
Seasoning to taste
1 tablespoonful toasted sesame seeds to garnish

1. Wash lentils and pick them over for stones. Place in a saucepan with the carrot, parsnip and bay leaf and cover with water. Bring to the boil, reduce the heat and simmer for about 40 minutes or until lentils are soft.

2. Heat the oil in a pan, add the onion and fry until soft — about 5 minutes. Add the mushrooms, herbs and tomato purée and cook for a further 2-3 minutes.

3. Combine together the lentil and mushroom mixtures, then either mash or purée in a blender or food processor until smooth. Taste and adjust the seasoning.

4. Turn into a serving dish and sprinkle with sesame seeds.

Serves 4.

VEGETABLE AND NUT PÂTÉ

2 tablespoonsful vegetable oil
1 medium onion, finely chopped
2 sticks of celery, finely chopped
1 medium carrot, grated
1 small parsnip, grated
3 oz (75g) fresh wholemeal breadcrumbs
3 oz (75g) peanuts, finely chopped or ground
½ teaspoonful dried mixed herbs
2 eggs, well beaten
Sea salt and freshly ground black pepper
2 bay leaves

To garnish:

Watercress
Tomato wedges

1. Heat the oil in a pan, add the onion and celery and fry until softened

2. Mix all the ingredients in a bowl, adding salt and pepper to taste.

3. Line the bottom of a 1 lb (450g) loaf tin with non-stick vegetable parchment or greaseproof paper. Spoon the mixture into the tin and press it down lightly. Arrange the bay leaves on top and cover with foil.

4. Place in a roasting dish half-filled with boiling water. Cook in a preheated moderate oven, 350°F/180°C

(Gas Mark 4) for about 1 hour. Leave to go cold in the tin, then turn out on to a plate. Serve garnished with watercress and wedges of tomato.

Serves 4.

BLACK OLIVE PÂTÉ

1 lb (450g) black olives, stoned
2 cloves of garlic, peeled and crushed
2 tablespoonsful olive oil
2 teaspoonsful dried oregano
Sea salt (optional)

To garnish:

1 hard-boiled egg

1. Place all the ingredients in a liquidizer or food processor and blend until smooth; check the seasoning.

2. Put into a pottery or earthenware serving dish.

3. For the garnish, separate the white and yolk of the hard-boiled egg; chop the white finely and sieve the yolk. Decorate the top of the dish with alternate rows of white and yolk.

Serves 6-8.

EGG AND ASPARAGUS PÂTÉ

1 lb (450g) fresh asparagus spears or
  10 oz (275g) tin
1 tablespoonful lemon juice
2 tablespoonsful natural yogurt
2 tablespoonsful single cream
4 hard-boiled eggs, chopped
Sea salt and freshly ground black pepper

To garnish:

Lemon slices
Chopped chives
Lettuce leaves to serve

1. Wash the asparagus well and using a sharp knife scrape from tip to base to remove any hard, woody parts. Trim stems to a uniform length and tie in a bundle.

2. Place upright in an asparagus kettle or tall, deep pan with enough boiling water to come halfway up the stems and cook for 15 minutes or until tender. Drain, reserve eight tips for decoration, chop the remainder, do likewise if using tinned asparagus.

3. Purée the chopped asparagus with the lemon juice, yogurt and cream in a liquidizer or food processor. Transfer to a bowl, add the eggs, seasoning and mix well.

4. Turn into four individual serving dishes or serve piled on to lettuce leaves. Garnish with lemon twists, chives and asparagus tips. Serve immediately.

Serves 4.

ADUKI BEAN PÂTÉ

---

6 oz (175g) aduki beans, soaked overnight
2 tablespoonsful tahini
2 tablespoonsful tamari
1 tablespoonful sesame oil
4-5 spring onions (white part only chopped)
1-2 tablespoonsful chopped chives to garnish
Seasoning to taste

1. Drain the aduki beans, place in a pan and cover with cold water. Bring to the boil and simmer gently for 45 minutes or until soft.

2. Drain, reserving ¼ pint (150ml) of the liquid.

3. Place the aduki beans in an electric blender or food processor with the tahini, tamari, oil, spring onions and reserved liquid. Blend to a soft creamy purée; taste and adjust the seasoning.

4. Turn into a serving dish and garnish with the chopped chives to serve.

Serves 4.

SPLIT PEA PÂTÉ

½ lb (225g) yellow split peas, soaked overnight and
*   drained*
14 oz (400g) tin tomatoes
Juice of ½ lemon
4 tablespoonsful vegetable oil
½ teaspoonful dried sage
1 clove of garlic, peeled and crushed
Sea salt and freshly ground black pepper
Pinch cayenne pepper

To garnish:

Lettuce leaves
Tomato wedges
Sprigs of parsley

1. Place the peas in a saucepan, cover them with plenty of fresh unsalted water and simmer for 30 minutes or until tender. Drain and cool.

2. Meanwhile, rub the tomatoes and their juice through a sieve to remove seeds. Place in a saucepan, bring to the boil and cook, uncovered, until reduced by two-thirds. Leave to cool.

3. Pass the peas through a sieve or use a food processor to make a purée. Beat into the tomato mixture, then stir in the lemon juice, oil, sage and garlic. Season with salt, pepper and cayenne pepper to taste. Cover and refrigerate until required.

4. Serve piled on crisp lettuce leaves, garnished with
    wedges of tomato and sprigs of parsley.

Serves 6-8.

CHESTNUT AND MUSHROOM PÂTÉ

½ lb (225g) chestnuts
1½ oz (40g) butter or polyunsaturated margarine
1 medium onion, finely chopped
2 sticks of celery, finely chopped
1 clove of garlic, peeled and crushed
½ lb (225g) mushrooms, sliced
1 oz (25g) wholemeal flour
¼ pint (150ml) vegetable stock
¼ pint (150ml) red wine
½ lb (225g) walnuts, ground
4 oz (100g) fresh wholemeal breadcrumbs
½-1 teaspoonful fresh sage, finely chopped
½-1 teaspoonful fresh thyme, finely chopped
½ teaspoonful paprika
1 tablespoonful tamari
2 eggs, beaten
Sea salt and freshly ground black pepper

1. Slit the chestnuts and cook in boiling water for about 30 minutes, or until soft. Drain, and while still warm, remove the outer shell and the inner skin. Chop coarsely and place in a bowl.

2. Melt butter in a large frying pan, add the onion, celery and garlic and fry until softened. Add the mushrooms and cook for a further 3-4 minutes.

3. Stir in the flour and cook for 1 minute. Gradually blend in the vegetable stock and wine. Heat stirring,

until sauce thickens, then remove from the heat. Add the remaining ingredients, seasoning with salt and pepper to taste. Mix thoroughly.

4. Grease a 2 lb (900g) loaf tin and line it with non-stick vegetable parchment or greaseproof paper. Fill with the mixture and bake in a preheated moderately hot oven, 375°F/190°C (Gas Mark 5) for 40-50 minutes or until firm to the touch. Allow to cool completely before removing the pâté from the tin.

Serves 6-8.

VEGETABLE TERRINE

2 lb (900g) spinach
1 tablespoonful olive oil
1½ oz (40g) butter
1 medium onion, finely chopped
1 small clove of garlic, peeled and crushed (optional)
¼ pint (150ml) single cream
3 oz (75g) fresh wholemeal breadcrumbs
3 eggs
1 egg yolk
Sea salt and freshly ground black pepper
Freshly grated nutmeg
2 medium carrots
6 oz (175g) broccoli florets
1 small red pepper
6 oz (175g) button mushrooms

1. Remove stalks from spinach and wash leaves. Heat
    the oil and butter in a large pan. Add the onion and
    garlic (if using) and fry until softened — about 5
    minutes.

2. Drain the spinach, add to the pan with just the water
    that clings to it. Cover the pan and cook the spinach
    over moderate heat, for 7-8 minutes, or until just
    tender, shaking the pan frequently to stop spinach
    from sticking. Remove the lid, lower the heat and
    continue cooking until any remaining liquid
    evaporates.

3. Put the spinach in a blender or food processor with the cream, breadcrumbs, whole eggs, egg yolk, and salt, pepper and nutmeg to taste and process until smooth.

4. Scrub carrots and cut them into matchsticks. Break broccoli into florets and cut off the stems. Cut pepper in half lengthwise, remove stalk, seeds and white pith. Cut this into strips. Wipe and trim the mushrooms.

5. Bring a pan of salted water to the boil, then one at a time, place the different vegetables in a blanching basket until tender. Drain and rinse under cold water. (Keep blanching water as a useful stock for a tasty vegetable soup.)

6. Line a 2 lb (900g) loaf tin or cast-iron terrine with vegetable parchment or greaseproof paper. Spread a layer of the spinach mixture in the base of the dish, then lay the strips of pepper on top. Make successive layers of the vegetables (one kind to a layer), separating each layer of vegetable with a layer of the spinach mixture.

7. Cover the terrine with a lid or buttered greaseproof paper. Stand in a roasting tin half-filled with boiling water. Cook in a moderate oven, 350°F/180°C (Gas Mark 4) for 1 hour. Remove from the oven and allow to cool in the terrine. Refrigerate overnight before unmoulding.

Serves 6-8.

COTTAGE CHEESE
AND VEGETABLE TERRINE

6 oz (175g) French beans
1 small red pepper
4 sticks of celery
2 large carrots
Sea salt
1½ lb (675g) natural cottage cheese
5 oz (150g) carton natural yogurt
¼ pint (150ml) thick mayonnaise (preferably home-made)
Freshly ground black pepper
2 teaspoonsful agar-agar
4 fl oz (120ml) water

1. Top and tail the beans. Cut pepper in half lengthwise and remove stalk, seeds and white pith. Cut into thin strips. Wash celery and trim sticks to an even thickness. Scrub carrots and cut into matchsticks.

2. Bring a pan of salted water to the boil. Parboil each vegetable separately until just tender — about 1-2 minutes for the French beans, 5 minutes for the carrots, 2 minutes for the celery and 2 minutes for the pepper — drain and rinse under cold water. Pat all the vegetables dry on kitchen paper and chill.

3. Bring the water to the boil, sprinkle in the agar-agar, stir briskly to dissolve and boil for 2 minutes.

4. Place the cottage cheese, yogurt and seasoning in a blender or food processor, then gradually pour in the dissolved agar-agar as you blend. When the mixture is completely smooth, add the mayonnaise.

5. Place a layer of the cheese mixture in the base of a 2 lb (900g) hinged loaf tin, then lay the strips of pepper on top. Cover with more of the cheese mixture and this time press the French beans into it. Repeat the layers with the pieces of celery and finally arrange the pieces of carrot along the length of the terrine, finishing with a layer of the cheese mixture. Spread top level with a spatula. Chill in the refrigerator for at least 4 hours or until set.

SPRING VEGETABLE TERRINE

A highly decorative terrine can be made by embedding pre-cooked vegetables of varied shapes and sizes in a velvety-rich savoury custard which is encased in leaves of spinach.

> ½ lb (225g) French beans
> 2 large straight carrots
> Sea salt
> 1 lb (450g) spinach
> 6 oz (175g) mushrooms
> 5 eggs
> 1 egg yolk
> ¾ pint (450ml) double cream
> 1 oz (25g) freshly grated Parmesan cheese
> Freshly ground black pepper
> Freshly grated nutmeg

1. Top and tail the beans. Scrub the carrots and cut into matchsticks. Bring a pan of salted water to the boil. Add the beans and cook for just 1 minute from when the water returns to the boil, then lift out and drain. Return the water to the boil, add the carrots and cook for 5 minutes, then lift out and drain.

2. Remove stalks from spinach and wash leaves. Blanch for 1 minute and spread the leaves out between layers of kitchen paper to absorb excess moisture. Wipe and trim the mushrooms.

3. Put the whole eggs, egg yolk and cream in a large heatproof bowl and beat thoroughly together. Stir

36

in the Parmesan cheese. Place the bowl over a pan of boiling water, making sure the bottom of the bowl does not touch the water. (If you have one, use a double boiler.) Cook, stirring constantly until the custard thickens and coats the back of a wooden spoon. Season with salt, pepper and freshly grated nutmeg to taste.

4. Lightly oil a 2 lb (900g) loaf tin or enamelled cast-iron terrine and spread out the leaves carefully inside as a thick lining, jigsawing together to leave no gaps.

5. Place the carrots in regular rows along the length of the terrine. Pour on the custard to submerge them completely. Cover the tin with foil or put on the lid and stand it in a roasting pan filled with water to reach half way up the terrine.

6. Cook in the centre of a preheated oven at 350°F/180°C (Gas Mark 4) for 25-30 minutes or until the custard is set. Continue in the same manner with the whole French beans and mushrooms, finishing with a layer of custard. Thus, the overall cooking time for this three-layer terrine should be about 1½ hours. Allow the terrine to cool completely before turning it out.

Variations: Substitute one or more of the following vegetables: artichoke bottoms, halved courgettes, broccoli florets, strips of green, red and yellow pepper or mange-tout peas.

Serves 6-8.

SOYA BEAN PÂTÉ

1 lb (450g) cooked soya beans
2 tablespoonsful vegetable oil
1 medium onion, finely chopped
2 sticks of celery, finely chopped
1 clove of garlic, peeled and crushed
⅓ pint (200ml) vegetable stock or milk
2 eggs
1 teaspoonful fresh rosemary, finely chopped
1 teaspoonful fresh thyme, finely chopped
1 tablespoonful fresh parsley, finely chopped
Sea salt and freshly ground black pepper
1 oz (25g) dry wholemeal bredcrumbs

To garnish:

Shredded lettuce
Sprigs of parsley
Tomato wedges

1. Purée the soya beans. Heat the oil in a pan, add the onion, celery and garlic and cook until soft but not browned. Add the soya beans and mix well.

2. Beat the eggs and vegetable stock or water together, add the herbs, salt and pepper, and stir into the soya bean mixture.

3. Grease a loaf tin with oil, sprinkle with the breadcrumbs and spoon in the mixture. Cover with kitchen foil and bake in a preheated hot oven at

400°F/200°C (Gas Mark 6) for 30 minutes or until firm. Allow to cool completely before removing from the tin.

4. Turn out onto a serving dish and surround with lettuce. Garnish with parsley and tomato.

Serves 6.

CLIVE BIRCH

GARLIC-MUSHROOM PÂTÉ

1 lb (450g) mushrooms
2 oz (50g) butter or polyunsaturated margarine
1 medium onion, finely chopped
4-5 cloves of garlic, peeled and crushed
1 tablespoonful yeast extract or miso
¼ pint (150ml) hot water
6 oz (175g) fresh wholemeal breadcrumbs
2-3 tablespoonsful lemon juice
1 tablespoonful fresh parsley, finely chopped
Sea salt and freshly ground black pepper
Freshly grated nutmeg to taste
Sprigs of fresh parsley to garnish

1. Wipe mushrooms, reserve 3 for garnishing, and chop remainder finely.

2. Melt the butter or margarine in a medium-sized saucepan. Add the onion and garlic and fry until soft but not browned — about 5 minutes. Add the mushrooms and cook for a further 2-3 minutes.

3. Dissolve the yeast extract or miso in the hot water. Add to the pan together with the breadcrumbs, lemon juice and parsley. Stir over low heat until most of the excess liquid has been evaporated. Season with salt, pepper and nutmeg to taste.

4. Spoon mixture equally into 4-6 individual ramekin dishes, cover and chill until ready to serve. Garnish with raw mushroom slices.

Serves 4-6.

EGG AND AVOCADO PÂTÉ

2 medium avocado pears, ripe to the touch
2 tablespoonsful lemon juice
4 hard-boiled eggs, finely chopped
2 tablespoonsful mayonnaise
1 small clove of garlic, peeled and crushed (optional)
1 tablespoonful fresh parsley, finely chopped
Sea salt and freshly ground black pepper

To garnish:

8 lettuce leaves
4 slices of lemon
4 sprigs of parsley

1. Cut the avocados in half (using a stainless steel knife) and remove the stones. Carefully scoop out the flesh into a bowl; reserve the shells.

2. Mash the avocado flesh with the lemon juice. Add the remaining ingredients, with salt and pepper to taste. Mix well, then spoon the mixture back into the avocado skins.

3. Line four individual serving dishes with the lettuce leaves. Place an avocado half on top and garnish each portion with a twist of lemon and a sprig of parsley. Serve at once.

Serves 4.

SAVOURY SPREADS

CURRIED CHEESE SPREAD/DIP

4 oz (100g) curd cheese
2 tablespoonsful mayonnaise
2 tablespoonsful yogurt
2 teaspoonsful curry powder
½ small onion, finely grated
Seasoning to taste

Mix all the ingredients together thoroughly. Use as a sandwich filler or serve in a bowl with raw vegetables for dipping.

MISO SPREAD

1 tablespoonful miso
3 tablespoonsful tahini
2 tablespoonsful water
1 tablespoonful vegetable oil
1 small onion, finely chopped
3 oz (75g) watercress, washed and trimmed
2 teaspoonsful tamari (real soya sauce)

1. Cream together the miso and tahini with the water to form a thick paste.

2. Heat the oil in a pan, add the onion and the chopped

watercress and fry until the onion is transparent.

3. Mix all the ingredients together and spread on wholemeal toast or bread.

RED KIDNEY BEAN SPREAD

6 oz (175g) cooked red kidney beans
4 oz (100g) Cheddar cheese, grated
2 teaspoonsful miso
½ level teaspoonful chilli powder (optional)
Seasoning
Chopped chives to garnish

1. Mash the beans or purée in a blender or food processor until smooth.

2. Combine all the ingredients and adjust the seasoning. Serve on slices of hot wholemeal toast sprinkled with the chives on top.

Serves 2-3.

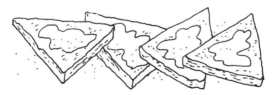

POTTED SPINACH

2 lb (900g) spinach
3 oz (75g) butter
1 small clove of garlic, peeled and crushed (optional)
4 fl oz (120g) double cream
Sea salt and freshly ground black pepper
Freshly grated nutmeg

1. Wash spinach well in several changes of water. Remove any coarse stalks. Place in a saucepan with only the water that clings to it. Cover and cook for 7 minutes. Drain thoroughly, then chop very finely or purée in a blender or food processor.

2. Melt 2 oz (50g) butter in a pan, add the garlic (if using) chopped spinach and cook gently until soft and pulpy. Remove from the heat and beat in the cream until smooth. Season with salt, pepper and nutmeg to taste.

3. Spoon the creamed spinach into individual ramekins or serving dishes. Leave to cool.

4. Melt remaining butter in a small pan, pour over top of spinach.

Note: This pâté will keep for a week if stored in the refrigerator, but does not freeze well.

Serves 6-8.

POTTED CHEESE WITH HERBS

It is possible to use any hard cheese or blue-veined cheese in this recipe or mix cheeses, so this is a practical way to use up leftover pieces of cheese. You can also use a different combination of herbs depending on what you have growing in the garden.

4 oz (100g) Cheddar cheese
1½ oz (40g) unsalted butter, softened
1 tablespoonful fresh parsley, chopped
1 tablespoonful fresh chervil, chopped
1 tablespoonful fresh thyme, chopped
Pinch ground mace
Freshly ground black pepper
1-2 tablespoonsful medium-dry sherry
Melted butter

1. Grate the cheese coarsely, add the butter and work in well. Add the herbs, mace and pepper to taste. Gradually work in the sherry until a firm paste is formed (the amount of sherry depends on the dryness of the cheese).

2. Press into small pots and seal the tops with a little butter. Cover with foil and refrigerate until required.

Note: This will keep in a refrigerator for 2-3 weeks or about 6 weeks in a freezer.

CREAM CHEESE
AND MUSHROOM SPREAD/DIP

½ lb (225g) button mushrooms
3 oz (75g) butter or polyunsaturated margarine
½ small onion, grated
4 oz (100g) cream cheese
Worcestershire sauce
Sea salt and freshly ground black pepper

1. Wipe mushrooms, reserve 3 for garnishing, and chop remainder finely.

2. Melt the butter or margarine in a pan. Add the mushrooms, grated onion and cook for 2-3 minutes until tender.

3. Put the mushroom and onion mixture into a blender or food processor together with the cream cheese, one or two drops of Worcestershire sauce, salt and pepper and process until smooth and creamy.

4. Pour the mixture equally into 4-6 small individual ramekin dishes, leave to cool. Refrigerate until ready to serve. Garnish with the reserved raw mushroom slices.

Serves 4-6.

MISO AND SPRING ONION SPREAD

6-7 spring onions, finely chopped
4 tablespoonsful tahini
1 tablespoonful miso
1 tablespoonful tamari

Combine all the ingredients together and use as a sandwich filling.

TAHINI AND MISO SPREAD

3 tablespoonsful tahini
3 tablespoonsful water
1 tablespoonful miso
Pinch of cayenne

Mix the ingredients together and spread on wholemeal bread or toast.

TAHINI AND TAMARI SPREAD

1 tablespoonful tahini
1 tablespoonful tamari
2 tablespoonsful water

Mix all the ingredients together and use as a sandwich filling. Garnish with chopped chives.

SUNFLOWER SEED SPREAD

6 oz (175g) sunflower seeds
2 oz (50g) butter, softened
1 tablespoonful tamari/shoyu
Seasoning to taste

1. Dry roast the seeds in a large, ungreased, frying pan over low heat, until just turning golden.

2. Grind the seeds as finely as possible in a food processor, nut mill or blender.

3. Put all the ingredients in a bowl and mix until smooth; check the seasoning.

SEED BUTTER

6 oz (175g) sunflower seeds
2 oz (50g) pumpkin seeds
4 tablespoonsful sunflower oil
2-3 tablespoonsful honey
4 oz (100g) tahini (sesame paste)

1. Grind the seeds as finely as possible in a blender, food processor or nut mill. Mix all the ingredients together well.

2. Put the seed butter into a 1 lb (450g) jam jar and screw down the lid or cover with cling film. Store in the refrigerator until ready to use.

Makes 1 lb (450g).

MUSHROOM PASTE

4 oz (100g) butter
1 medium onion, finely chopped
1-2 cloves of garlic, peeled and crushed
2 lb (900g) mushrooms, roughly chopped
Sea salt and freshly ground black pepper
Pinch cayenne pepper
2 eggs, well beaten
1 tablespoonful brandy (optional)
Melted butter

1. Melt the butter in a large pan, add the onion and garlic and fry until softened.

2. Add the mushrooms and season with salt, pepper and cayenne pepper to taste. Cover the pan and leave to simmer gently for 15 minutes or until mushrooms are tender, shaking the pan from time to time. Liquidize the contents of the pan in a blender or food processor.

3. Return the mixture to a clean pan. Add the eggs and cook over a gentle heat until the mixture thickens, stirring all the time. Do not boil.

4. Stir in the brandy. Pot into small ramekin dishes and when cold pour a little melted butter over the top to seal the paste. Store in the refrigerator.

PEANUT BUTTER

5 oz (150g) shelled roasted peanuts
Vegetable oil (if needed)
Sea salt

1. Grind peanuts in an electric blender or food processor in short bursts, regulating the time according to whether you want a smooth or crunchy butter. Help the mixture onto the blades with a spatula, with the motor off; adding oil as necessary, until peanut butter is the consistency you want. (Food processors do an efficient job of making peanut butter. If you do have one, you may not need any extra oil.)

2. Add salt to taste and store the butter in a jar.

Note: Any kinds of nuts either raw or roasted can be made into a butter by grinding them in a blender, food processor or nut mill. Try cashews, hazelnuts, walnuts, Brazils, pecans, pistachios and almonds, or use a mixture of different kinds of nuts. The ground nuts can also be mashed with the oil by hand to produce a butter of the consistency you like.

Makes 6 oz (175g).

LENTIL PASTE

1 small onion
1 oz (25g) butter
4 oz (100g) brown lentils
½ pint (275ml) vegetable stock or water
2 oz (50g) fresh wholemeal breadcrumbs
1 teaspoonful yeast extract
1 teaspoonful dried mixed herbs
Seasoning
Melted butter

1. Peel and grate the onion and cook in the butter for
   a few minutes. Add the lentils and stock and cook
   until soft and all the liquid has been absorbed.

2. Reduce the cooked lentils to a purée by mashing or
   sieving. Add the breadcrumbs, yeast extract, herbs,
   and seasoning to taste. Leave to cool.

3. Store in a jar, covered with a layer of melted butter.
   This will keep for several days in the refrigerator.

PARTY DIPS

MEXICAN BEAN DIP

---

14 oz (400g) tin red kidney beans
¼ pint (150ml) soured cream
4 oz (100g) cream cheese
1 tomato, skinned, deseeded and chopped
1 stick of celery, finely chopped
1 small clove of garlic, peeled and crushed
1 small onion, finely chopped
2 tablespoonful red pepper, chopped
½ teaspoonful ground coriander
¼ teaspoonful chilli powder
¼ teaspoonful dried oregano
2 teaspoonsful tarragon vinegar
Sea salt and freshly ground black pepper

1. Mash the beans and their liquid with the soured cream, or purée in a blender.

2. Add the remaining ingredients and mix well. Taste and adjust the seasoning.

3. Pour into a serving bowl, cover and place in the refrigerator to blend flavours. Serve with crisp tortillas and crudités for dipping.

Serves 6-8.

CRUDITÉS

Crudités are a selection of raw vegetables cut into thin strips which can be dipped into your dips or pâtés or eaten on their own.

The following vegetables are suitable:

Carrots	Spring onions
Celery	Cauliflower
Peppers	Radishes
Fennel	Mushrooms
Cucumber	

CHEESE AND CELERY DIP

2 oz (50g) butter
½ lb (225g) Cheddar cheese, finely grated
¼ pint (150ml) single cream
1 level teaspoonful made mustard
2 sticks of celery, finely chopped
Sea salt and freshly ground black pepper
1 oz (25g) salted peanuts, roughly chopped

1. Beat the butter until creamy with a wooden spoon.

2. Gradually work in the cheese then stir in the cream, mustard, celery and salt and pepper to taste.

3. Transfer to a serving bowl and sprinkle with peanuts.

Serves 4-6.

TOFU GUACAMOLE

10 oz (275g) tofu
2 large ripe avocado pears
2 tablespoonsful lemon juice
1 small onion, finely chopped
1 clove of garlic, peeled and crushed (optional)
2 teaspoonsful tamari
3 tablespoonsful olive oil
Pinch cayenne pepper
Sea salt and freshly ground black pepper

1. Drain the tofu and cut into cubes. Place in a mixing bowl.

2. Halve the avocados and remove the stones. Scoop the flesh into the bowl and sprinkle with lemon juice to prevent browning. Add the onion, garlic, if using, tamari, oil and seasoning to taste. Beat thoroughly until smooth and turn into a serving dish.

3. Serve the dip with a selection of prepared, crisp raw vegetables — for example, carrots, cauliflower and celery — and small savoury biscuits or crisps.

Serves 4-6.

GARLIC MAYONNAISE DIP

4 large cloves of garlic
2 egg yolks
½ level teaspoonful mustard powder
Sea salt and freshly ground black pepper
¼ pint (150ml) olive oil
2 teaspoonsful hot water
1 tablespoonful lemon juice

1. Peel the cloves of garlic and place them in a blender goblet. Add the egg yolks, mustard and seasoning to taste.

2. Process until smooth, then remove centre cap and pour the oil in a thin, steady stream through the hole in the lid. Do not switch off the motor while oil is being added. When about half of the oil has been incorporated, the rest may be added a little more quickly.

3. Add the hot water and lemon juice and process for a few seconds. Taste and adjust the seasoning. Pour into a serving dish and chill. Serve with crisp raw vegetables for dipping.

Note: Ensure that all the ingredients are at room temperature.

Serves 4-6.

YOGURT AND CUCUMBER DIP

½ cucumber, coarsely grated
½ lb (225g) carton natural yogurt
1-2 cloves of garlic, peeled and crushed
½ level teaspoonful dill seed (optional)
1 teaspoonful white wine vinegar
2 teaspoonsful olive oil
Sea salt and freshly ground black pepper

Combine all of the dip ingredients in a bowl adding salt and pepper to taste; mix well. Chill before serving.

Serves 6-8.

ARTICHOKE DIP

14 oz (400g) tin artichoke hearts, drained
4 tablespoonsful olive oil
1 tablespoonful cider vinegar
2 teaspoonsful lemon juice
1 teaspoonful dried oregano
Sea salt and freshly ground black pepper

1. Place all the ingredients in a blender or food processor and purée until smooth and creamy. Season to taste.

2. Turn dip into a bowl and surround with fingers of crisp vegetables — carrot, celery, etc.

Serves 4.

GUACAMOLE
(Mexican Avocado Dip)

2 large ripe avocado pears
Juice of ½ lemon
½ small onion, peeled and finely grated
2 tomatoes, skinned, deseeded and chopped
1 clove of garlic, peeled and crushed (optional)
1 tablespoonful fresh coriander or parsley, finely
  chopped
2 tablespoonsful vegetable oil
1 teaspoonful chilli powder
Sea salt and freshly ground black pepper

1. Halve the avocados and remove the stones. Scoop the
   flesh into a bowl and mash with the lemon juice to
   prevent browning.

2. Add the remaining ingredients and beat thoroughly
   until smooth. Season with salt and pepper to taste.

3. Serve the guacamole in a small dish in the centre of
   a plate, arrange crudités round the edge for dipping.

Note: Very ripe avocado pears, suitable for mashing, are
often sold cheaply.

Serves 4.

TAHINI DIP

4 heaped tablespoonsful tahini
1-2 cloves of garlic, peeled and crushed (optional)
1 tablespoonful tamari/shoyu
2-3 tablespoonsful lemon juice
1 tablespoonful chives chopped
Little water if needed

1. Combine all the ingredients in a bowl and beat to a creamy consistency. Thin with a little water if needed.

2. Serve with warm wholemeal pitta bread and crisp vegetable crudités. Sprinkle with chopped chives.

Variation: Mix ¼ pint (150ml) yogurt and tahini in a small bowl. Add chives, garlic and lemon juice to taste.

TOFU DIP

5 oz (150g) tofu
Juice of ½ lemon
3 tablespoonsful vegetable oil
1 teaspoonful tamari
½ teaspoonful sea salt
3-4 spring onions, finely chopped
2 tablespoonsful fresh parsley, finely chopped

1. Drain the tofu. Place in a bowl, add the rest of the ingredients and beat thoroughly until thick and creamy.

2. Serve chilled with a sprinkling of parsley. Will keep in the refrigerator for a few days. Stir before serving.

Note: This basic recipe can be adapted in a countless number of ways by adding one or more of the following ingredients: curry powder, tahini, cider vinegar, tomato purée, onion and/or garlic (minced), chives, dried herbs, mustard, etc. The choice is yours.

HUMMUS

Hummus is a protein rich dip of Middle Eastern origin. It tastes best eaten with pittas — unleavened bread — or you can serve it with wholemeal toast rather like a pâté.

½ lb (225g) chick peas, soaked overnight
3-4 cloves of garlic, peeled and crushed
4 tablespoonsful tahini
Juice of 1-2 lemons
3 tablespoonsful olive oil
1 teaspoonful sea salt

To garnish:

Chopped parsley
Paprika
Black olives

1. Drain the chick peas, place in a pan and cover with cold water. Bring to the boil and simmer gently for 2-2½ hours until soft.

2. Drain, reserving ¼ pint (150ml) of the liquid. Place the chick peas in a liquidizer or food processor with the tahini, garlic, lemon juice, oil, salt and reserved liquid and blend at high speed until smooth. (Alternatively, pound the chick peas and garlic to a paste with a pestle and mortar. Add the tahini, lemon juice, and oil beating in each amount until blended. Add seasoning to taste and adjust the consistency of the hummus by adding a little of the cooking liquid.)

3. Spoon the mixture into a serving dish and chill until required. Garnish with chopped parsley, paprika and black olives, if liked. Serve with warm wholemeal pitta bread and sticks of raw vegetables.

Serves 6-8.

BLUE STILTON AND AVOCADO DIP

4 oz (100g) blue Stilton cheese, crumbled
¼ pint (150ml) soured cream
1 large ripe avocado pear
Juice of ½ lemon
2 oz (50g) walnuts, ground
Sea salt and freshly ground black pepper

1. Mash the cheese with a fork and stir in the soured cream.

2. Halve the avocado and remove the stone. Scoop the flesh into a bowl and mash with the lemon juice, add to the cheese mixture with the walnuts and salt and pepper to taste. Mix well.

3. Serve dip with a selection of savoury biscuits and raw vegetables, such as red and green pepper, carrot, celery, cucumber and cauliflower florets.

Serves 4-6.

AUBERGINE DIP

2 large aubergines (about 1½ lb/675g)
1 tablespoonful lemon juice
1 clove of garlic, peeled and crushed
2 tablespoonsful olive oil
2 tablespoonsful fresh parsley, chopped
Sea salt and freshly ground black pepper

1. Prick the aubergines all over with a fork. Bake in a preheated moderately hot oven, 375°F/190°C (Gas Mark 5), for 40-50 minutes until softened. Cool, then peel off the skin.

2. Put the flesh into a bowl and mash with a fork. Add the garlic and lemon juice, olive oil and parsley and mix well; taste and season. (Alternatively, chop flesh coarsely then put into a blender or food processor. Add the remaining ingredients and blend until smooth and creamy. Season to taste.)

3. Turn into a serving dish, cover with cling film and refrigerate until well chilled. Serve garnished with chopped parsley.

Serves 4.

INDEX

63